NORTHERN SPOTTED OWLS

A TRUE BOOK

by

Patricia A. Fink Martin

ϕ

Children's Press®

A Division of Scholastic Inc.

New York Toronto London Auckland Sydney
Mexico City New Delhi Hong Kong

Northern spotted owl

Reading Consultant
Nanci R. Vargus, Ed.D.
*Primary Multiage Teacher
Decatur Township Schools,
Indianapolis, IN*

Content Consultant
Kathy Carlstead, Ph.D.
Honolulu Zoo

Dedication:
*To my daughter,
Leslie Sara Martin*

The photograph on the cover
shows a northern spotted owl.
The photograph on the title
page shows an owl swooping
down to catch its prey.

Library of Congress Cataloging-in-Publication Data

Martin, Patricia A. Fink.
    Northern spotted owls / by Patricia A. Fink Martin.
        p.   cm. — (A True Book)
    Includes bibliographical references and index.
    Summary: Describes the life cycle, characteristics, habitats, and behav-
iors of Northern spotted owls, as well as ways to prevent their extinction.
    ISBN 0-516-22164-7 (lib. bdg.)   0-516-27474-0 (pbk.)
    1. Spotted owl—Northwest, Pacific—Juvenile literature. 2. Endangered
species—Northwest, Pacific—Juvenile literature. [1. Spotted owl. 2. Owls.
3. Endangered species.] I. Title. II. Series.
598.9'7—dc21   2001032295

Contents

A northern spotted owl sits in a tree, searching for its next meal.

A Night-Time Hunter

Night fell on the forest. Tall trees with wide trunks cast dark shadows in the moonlight. On the forest floor, a small woodrat picked through the leaves in search of something to eat. It often fed at night because that's when it felt safe from most **predators**.

Suddenly, the woodrat felt a rush of wind on its face. As it looked up, it saw huge, sharp **talons** coming toward it. The owner of those claws flew on wide wings that spread almost 4 feet (1.2 meters) across. Big owl eyes stared at its next meal.

Who is this hunter that flies at night? It's the northern spotted owl. Like most owls, this hunter has a round, pie-shaped face. Large brown eyes sit on top of its small yellow bill. White dots, spots, and splotches mark its chocolate brown feathers. This owl stands about 18 inches (46 centimeters) tall.

The northern spotted owl
lives on the west coast of
the United States.

Three types of spotted owls hunt in the forests of western North America. The northern spotted owl can be found in forests along the coasts of British Columbia, Washington, Oregon, and northern California. The California spotted owl and Mexican spotted owl live in southern California and Mexico.

There's No Place

The northern spotted owl lives in special old-growth forests.

The northern spotted owl makes its home in a very special forest. This forest isn't like most forests you may have visited. The northern spotted owl lives in an **old-growth**, or ancient, **forest.**

Here the trees grow wide and tall. Many of the tree trunks measure 6 to 7 feet (1.8 to 2.1 m) across. You would need two or three friends to help you give these tree trunks a hug! These wooden giants reach 100 to 200 feet (30 to 60 m) into the sky. Many have stood here for hundreds of years. All year round, their needles shade the forest floor.

Like Home

This young girl shows just how giant these trees really are.

Trees in old-growth forests may reach 200 feet (60 m) tall.

The forest floor catches fallen leaves and trees. Mosses and mushrooms cover the rotting wood. Some trees don't fall after they die. They remain standing and are called **snags**.

A Spotted Owl's Day

As your day begins, the spotted owl's day ends. The spotted owl is **nocturnal**. This means that the owl hunts at night. As the sun rises, the owl returns to its favorite tree to rest.

If you were to visit the spotted owl's forest home,

An owl rests in a tree until nightfall.

you would probably have trouble finding the owl. Where is it hiding? Look high above you. Spotted owls often **roost** on limbs 100 feet (30 m) in the air. Search carefully, for their dark feathers blend well against the tree trunks.

You could try calling to it. The spotted owl is very curious. Sound out *hoo-hoo-hoo-hoo*. The owl might answer. It might even come down to take a look at you!

With its brown splotched coat, the northern spotted owl blends into the trees.

An owl flies quietly through the trees.

When the sun sets, the spotted owl rises from its perch. It beats its wings quickly, and then glides through the trees. It searches for food. Each spotted owl hunts in its own home area. Sometimes the owl flies many miles to find food.

The northern spotted owl eats small mammals. Its favorite meal is a flying squirrel. The hunter looks for food on the forest floor and in the trees. When it spots a meal, it

This owl is about to grab its prey with its sharp talons.

grabs its victim with its powerful talons. After making a kill, the spotted owl swallows its **prey** whole. Several hours later, it coughs up a bundle of fur and bones.

Owl Ears and Eyes

Imagine hunting at night in the forest. Does it sound like a hard thing to do? It would be for us, but it's not hard for the spotted owl. Its special eyes and ears help it find food in the dark. The spotted owl's large eyes gather extra light. This helps

An owl can spot its prey from a high branch.

the bird see better at night.
The white feathers around its
eyes help too. They reflect
light into the owl's eyes.

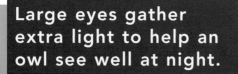
Large eyes gather extra light to help an owl see well at night.

A nocturnal hunter must use its ears too. But where are its ears? The spotted owl doesn't have any outside, or external, ears. Even so, it does hear very well! You can find openings to its internal ears hidden under its feathers.

As the spotted owl listens, it twists its head. It moves its head up and down and back and forth. The owl lifts its feathers over its ears. Even its pie-shaped face helps the owl.

An owl can twist its head so that it is looking backward.

The shape of an owl's face
helps funnel sounds to its ears.

Its face acts like a funnel to catch sound.

The spotted owl hears many things. It can hear the wind whistling through the treetops. It can hear a small cricket calling for a mate. It can even hear the scratching of a squirrel's sharp nails on a tree trunk.

Raising Baby Owlets

A young owl spends most of
its nights hunting, and it
rests during the day. But
after its third year, it takes
on another job. Almost every
March, it raises a family of
young owlets. Early in the
year, young adults begin
looking for mates. Older

26

Adult owls find their mates in early spring.

owls find their mates from last year. Spotted owls mate for life.

Each pair searches for a nest. Spotted owls don't build their own nests. Some might borrow old nests from large birds like hawks, while others nest in the tops of trees or in a clump of mistletoe. Still others nest in tree holes.

The female lays two or three white eggs. She sits on them to keep them warm. She never leaves them, even to get food. Her mate hunts for her, and brings food to the nest site.

This pair of owls searches for an empty nest to use.

Inside each egg, a baby owlet grows. The eggs take a month to hatch. The young

A young owlet stays in its nest for several weeks (right). The owlet gets food from its parent (below).

birds stay in the nest for several weeks. The parents feed them small pieces of meat.

Soon the owlet must leave the nest and live on its own.

Soon they learn to fly and hunt for food. By fall, they will leave the nest for good, in search of their own place in the forest.

Endangered

Many young owls don't live long. Predators kill many owlets. Others can't find enough food and they starve to death.

Each year, fewer young northern spotted owls make it to adulthood. In 1990, the United States government declared the northern spotted

Many young owls do not survive to adulthood.

owl an **endangered species**.
No one can hunt or harm a
northern spotted owl.

It's not just the owl that is in danger—its forest home is also disappearing fast. Timber companies want the big trees,

Many large forests have been completely destroyed.

so they hire workers called **loggers** to cut them down. They sell the wood to build houses and make furniture.

The northern spotted owl needs this special forest. It can't live in other types of forests for two reasons. First, the big trees provide cover from predators. Second, most of the animals that the spotted owl eats live only in the old-growth forest. These small prey are not plentiful. To find enough to eat, an owl needs lots of forest to hunt in!

The northern spotted owl has other problems too. The barred owl has begun to take over its home. This invader competes

with the spotted owl for food, nest sites, and space. The northern spotted owl seldom fights the invader. It simply gives in and moves to another area of the forest.

Can They Be Saved?

In 1991, a judge ruled that both the northern spotted owl and its home must be protected. No more trees could be cut down in these forests. A special group began to study the problem.

In the early 1990s, few trees were cut in old-growth forests. This caused some loggers to

The northern spotted owl and some of its territory are protected by the courts.

lose their jobs. The loggers and their families protested the judge's ruling. They complained that the government favored owls over loggers.

Finally, the judge ruled that the timber companies could cut the trees, but they must leave some big ones alone. Trees around spotted owl nesting and roosting sites could not be cut down.

Will the loggers leave enough trees? Can the spotted

A woman protests the cutting down of old-growth forests.

owl survive? Some people are worried. They say that isn't enough to protect the owls.

Help Save the Spotted Owl

What can you do to help the northern spotted owl? You can read other books about the spotted owl and old-growth forests. Tell others what you have learned. Join a group that helps endangered animals. Or, find one that's working to protect America's forests. You can also help raise money for their projects. Does your father or mother like to build things from wood? Then help them choose the lumber. Find out where it comes from. If the wood comes from old-growth forests, don't buy it! Help save these special forests and the animals that live there.

To Find Out More

If you'd like to find out more about the spotted owl and old-growth forests, check out the following resources.

 **Books**

George, Jean Craighead. **There's an Owl in My Shower.** HarperCollins Publishers, 1995.

Guiberson, Brenda Z. **Spotted Owl: Bird of the Ancient Forest.** Henry Holt, 1994.

Silverstein, Alvin, Virginia Silverstein, and Robert Silverstein. **The Spotted Owl.** Millbrook Press, 1994.

Siy, Alexander. **Ancient Forests.** Macmillan, 1991.

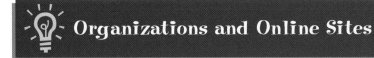

Organizations and Online Sites

Earth Observatory: Spotting the Spotted Owl, by John Weier
http://128.183.201.7/Study /SpottedOwls/

Owls of the World
http://www.owlpages.com/ species/spotted/index.html

Save America's Forests
4 Library Court, SE
Washington, DC 20003
http://saveamerica's forests.org

The Wilderness Society
900 Seventeenth St. NW
Washington, DC 20006-2596
http://wilderness.org

Important Words

endangered species a kind of animal that is in danger of dying out

logger a man or woman whose job is cutting down trees in a forest

nocturnal active at night

old-growth forest a natural forest that has many fallen, rotting logs, dead, standing trees, and a mix of young and old trees. It is also called an ancient forest.

predator an animal that kills other animals for food

prey an animal hunted and eaten by another animal

roost to rest or sleep on a high perch

snag a dead, standing tree that is often home to a number of birds

talon a sharp claw of a bird of prey

Index

Meet the Author

Patricia A. Fink Martin holds a doctorate in biology. After spending many years teaching and working in the laboratory, she began writing science books for children. In 1998, *Booklist* chose her first book, *Animals that Walk on Water*, as one of the ten best animal books for children for that year. She has since published eight more books. Dr. Martin lives in Tennessee with her husband Jerry, their daughter Leslie, and their golden retriever Ginger.